Please Give a Devotion

Amy Bolding

BAKER BOOK HOUSE
Grand Rapids, Michigan 49506

Paperback edition issued 1982

ISBN: 0-8010-0819-0

Eleventh printing, October 1995

Printed in the United States of America

THIS BOOK IS LOVINGLY DEDICATED
TO MY HUSBAND, WHO LIVES TO HELP
OTHERS.

CONTENTS

1

Steps

"The steps of a good man are ordered by the Lord: and he delighteth in his way." — Psalm 37:23
"For now thou numberest my steps." — Job 14:16

Have you ever watched a young couple teaching their baby to walk? They stand or sit a few feet apart and with the very gentlest words entice the little one to take a few steps, from one to the other. How elated they are when the baby at last turns loose and makes those few short steps alone. They hug the child and the baby is happy because he has pleased them. The parents are happy because their child is developing.

Sometimes in life we have sickness and troubles which cause us to have to learn to walk again. A lady, well in her sixties, broke both legs in a car wreck. After many weeks without walking she was told she could start walking again.

"Oh I am afraid I will never learn to walk again," she exclaimed to the nurse.

"How foolish, of course you will learn," the nurse told her, "You learned the first time, and you were not nearly so large as now."

The funny thought, of how she must have learned to walk

as a baby, made the lady laugh. Soon she was trying to walk again.

As new Christians we are eager to walk with God. We try to serve Him and walk as He would want us to. Sad to say sometimes Christians make mistakes and must learn to walk with God all over again. How wonderful that He is so patient and kind to help us when we falter.

"The steps of a good man are ordered of the Lord." Have you at times questioned a move you had to make, or a loss you sustained? If you thought of the fact that God ordered your footsteps you were content to wait and see what He had in store for you.

My husband told me the story of a boy who was with his outfit during World War II.

Joe's duty was to wait on the Captain of his company. Making camp was no easy task. Making camp for himself and the Captain was a long tedious job. Joe had just finished digging two slit-trenches, putting in the bed rolls and was ready to, as they said, "hit the sack."

A super secret message came from battalion headquarters. The message was to be sent on to the flank of the adjacent company.

The day had been long and very tiring. The men in the company were all at their posts, busy.

"I am sorry, Joe, but I will have to send you with this message." The Captain realized he was asking the boy to perform a task, above and beyond his call of duty.

Joe started off with dragging steps, a tired droop to his shoulders. He grumbled as he passed the Chaplain's trench.

While Joe was gone a mortar barrage came in. Returning sometime later Joe found one of the shells had made a direct hit on his bed. But for the grace of God, in calling him out to an unsavory duty, he would have been in that slit-trench bed. How he thanked God for taking him out of the way! Many times we are kept from dangers we do not know about because "The steps of a good man are ordered of the Lord."

STEPS

I know not where his islands lift
Their fronded palms in air;
I only know I cannot drift
Beyond His love and care.
—John Greenleaf Whittier

How safe a Christian should feel, knowing God has numbered every step. Knowing He cares when we come to an obstacle too hard for us to cross. Knowing how often we stumble by the way. Often we walk with small children. When little legs grow tired or we come to a step too high for the child, we merely lift the little one up with an easy swing and set him down again in a level spot. Our Heavenly Father holds our hand and when our steps grow weak and we wonder how we will get along, up we go and over. God has a way and ways we cannot see but He is there to guide our steps.

MY SAVIOUR

The Saviour placed from heaven above
His wonderous claim on me,
And I surrendered to His love
That day His own to be.

The Lord is all I ever need,
His best He will supply;
With manna He my soul will feed,
On Him I can rely.

He is my life, my everything;
He is my all-in-all;
He makes my weary heart to sing,
He answers when I call.

With Christ I walk along life's way
In fellowship divine;
And it's enough for me each day
To know that He is mine.
—J. T. Bolding

In this life we may expect to find many different kinds of steps.

There will be difficult steps. God will help you climb them. There will be fearful steps. God can calm our fears. There will be misunderstood steps. Families and friends do not always understand why we spend time working for our church and our Lord, when we might be making a little more money. There will be steps when it seems as if "the wicked prosper." There will be sinful steps. God is faithful and just to forgive us our sins if we confess them and ask forgiveness.

Whatever your steps may be, if you are a child of God you have the blessed assurance of Psalms 37:23: "The steps of a good man are numbered of the Lord."

2

Viewpoint of Life

"Blessed is the man that walketh not in the counsel of the ungodly, nor standeth in the way of sinners, nor sitteth in the seat of the scornful. But his delight is in the law of the Lord; and in his law doth he meditate day and night." — Psalm 1:1-2

One time my husband and I spent a whole day looking at the Grand Canyon in Arizona. We were not alone. Hundreds of others were looking at the canyon also. There were many viewpoints from which to look. We did not stand in one spot all the time. Each viewpoint gave a different aspect of the great wonder of nature.

Often during the day we used our field glasses to help us see further away. Some people were riding horses in order to go down into the canyon.

Never will we forget the beauty and wonder of the things we saw that day. As we drove away late in the afternoon we wondered how anyone could see such handiwork of God's creation and fail to believe on Him.

As the Psalmist said so long ago, "Blessed is the man who meditates on God's law."

We have our own choice of viewpoints in life to make. The choice we make determines so many things.

Two men trod the way of life;
The first, with downcast eye;
The second, with an eager face
Uplifted to the sky.

He who gazed upon the ground
Said, "Life is dull and gray."
But he who looked into the stars
Went singing on his way.

"I have a right to choose my own viewpoint," people are apt to say. But is it right to choose a viewpoint in life which will hurt others? A grandmother told me a sad story. Her son and his wife were very faithful about attending church and Sunday School. Their two small children were happy and well adjusted in their classes. Then something trivial happened which made the parents angry. They said ugly things about the church and stopped going.

When the grandmother made a long trip to visit the little family, she was disturbed to find her two grandchildren being taught a bitter attitude toward sacred things.

One day, when she was alone with the six year old boy, she asked if he knew who Jesus was. The little child went to his room, opened a drawer where he kept his treasures. Coming back he held out a Sunday School card. On the card was a picture of Christ and the children of the world. He pointed to Christ in the picture.

"He is the man in the picture," the child automatically dropped his voice, "We used to go and hear about him but now we do not talk about him any more."

The grandmother, a devout Christian, left that home with a broken heart. All her pleading could not make her son and his wife see that their wrong viewpoint was harmful to their children.

With so many parents taking wrong viewpoints of life today, is it any wonder we hear the cry on every hand, "delinquent children"?

The majority of people live as if they had all the time in the world to make their viewpoint right.

16

VIEWPOINT OF LIFE

Young people often say, "Let me look at life through pleasure's eyes while I am young." But sometimes pleasure demands a very high price.

A High School senior in our neighborhood wanted only to have fun and be popular. One afternoon, against the wishes of her mother, she went out riding with a group of young people. The small car, in which they were riding was overloaded. The young people were having fun and racing another car. Suddenly there was a wreck. The driver of the car was killed. The High School Senior was paralyzed from her neck down. The viewpoint of having only fun was changed to a viewpoint of helplessness and unhappiness.

Some people look at life from the viewpoint of greed. They forget there are many things more precious than silver or gold.

Then we might think of other viewpoints: such as pessimism, the viewpoint of optimism, the viewpoint of living for others, and the viewpoint of making the world more beautiful.

Hilda Butler Farr had an optimistic attitude when she wrote the following poem.

TOMORROW'S OPPORTUNITY

If we might have a second chance
　　To live the days once more,
And rectify mistakes we've made
　　To even up the score.

If we might have a second chance
　　To use the knowledge gained,
Perhaps we might become at last
　　As fine as God ordained.

But though we can't retrace our steps,
　　However stands the score,
Tomorrow brings another chance
　　For us to try once more.

Oh how much happier are the ones who look at life from

the viewpoint of the Christian. They have only to read the Scriptures to see the way God would have them go.

The Bible is filled with promises for those who have the viewpoint of following Christ. Such a viewpoint will bring a peace that passeth all understanding.

3

God's Stairway

"Wherefore He is able also to save them to the utter-most that come unto God by him, seeing he ever liveth to make intercession for them. . . . For such an high priest became us, who is holy, harmless, undefiled, separate from sinners, and made higher than the heavens; Who needeth not daily to offer up sacrifice, first for his own sins, and then for the people's: for this he did once, when he offered up himself." — Hebrews 7:25-28

Someone has said, "God has His own secret stairway into every heart." Yes there is a way in which different hearts respond to the Heavenly Father. My father was for many years a country preacher. At one of his churches a dear old lady had the shouting kind of religion. She was sure to shout praises to the Lord when a new soul was born into the kingdom of God.

When I was a young girl attending a small denominational college, I saw one day in chapel the singing kind of religion. We were having our annual spring revival. One of the most popular boys on the football team, walked down the aisle and gave his heart to Christ. An older student, a minister, started singing, "Oh Happy Day." Soon all the students were singing and more were walking down the aisle. The services lasted two hours. From one old song to another the students sang. Some went to their friends and asked them to trust Christ. Many young people truly found a way to God's heart that day.

Many years later I was privileged to be in a service where we could almost look up the stairway into heaven. W. A. Criswell, pastor of the first Baptist Church, Dallas, Texas, was a guest speaker. The convention hall was filled with ministers and lay workers from all over the state. Just at the close of his wonderful message, a young minister in the back of the building started shouting. He left his place, went down the aisle, shouting all the way, praises to God. Soon all the congregation started saying Amen, and singing. Needless to say those workers went home that day with new visions of God's glory and power. A spirit of revival broke out all over our state.

In the book of Hebrews the writer seems to have found a way to God, through Jesus Christ.

A few years back a great furor was started by an article which was published in a magazine with nationwide circulation. This article said unkind and, most of us felt, untrue things about our Sunday schools and churches. The people over the land wrote letters of protest. They talked to each other, but the controversy was soon forgotten.

Religion is an inward concept and fellowship with God. Religion is personal and must be real if it is worth anything to the individual. Religion is a way of life and a power dwelling within us to help us live that way of life. Although I might feel my mother was the best Christian I knew, her goodness will not open the stairway to God for me. I may long to be religious for the sake of my child or my friend, but since religion is a relationship between the individual and God I can only know the way for myself. There are people who will find the way if we but direct them. Religion is a standard for life and a power within us to help us reach that standard.

GOD'S STAIRWAY

As a child, when my mother read Bible stories I liked very much to hear her read the story of Jacob's ladder. I could picture a beautiful stairway with brass rails, shining lights, and angels on the steps. There at the top a great shining throne. I do not know how that stairway looked to poor homesick Jacob that night, but I can know the stairway that leads from my heart to the throne of God.

The first step on my stairway was the step of a surrendered heart. At a very early age I gave my heart to Christ. I was such a little girl the minister thought I could not possibly know what it meant to trust Christ. I was sent back to my seat and ignored. But God did not ignore me. From that day until this I have had the knowledge of His love and of being His child.

The next step on the stairway from the heart to the throne of God is a surrendered life. The joy of being accepted into church fellowship and the feeling of being a part of God's body of believers goes with a surrendered life.

A surrendered heart and life are the foundation steps, but there are other important steps to build if your stairway would lead to God's throne.

The step of prayer, talking with God daily is so precious to a child of God. How can anyone ever have a stairway to God's throne without a prayer life.

WHAT IS BEST?

You wonder what is best?
Then place the matter in His hands
And leave to him the rest,
The load is lifted when you pray;
Your heart will loose its sigh
When you give all unto His hands
  As He is standing by.
                    —Author unknown

Our prayer life must be more real than that of two small boys. They slipped away from the Sunday School teacher and made a tour around the sanctuary. When the boys returned to class the overworked teacher asked.

"Where have you boys been?"

"Oh we have been upstairs praying," Bill told her quickly.

"Now Bill don't lie about it." The other little fellow said.

The teacher wisely dropped the subject.

Then of course no stairway to God could be complete without a step of service. We long to be of service to those we love. If we truly love God we will find ways to serve Him.

THE STEWARDSHIP OF GIVING

God loaned me a life and I must pay
Him back a portion of each day
In loving service; I must give
A part of every hour I live
In thoughtful, kindly deeds to others
Who are my sisters and my brothers.

God loaned me coins I may not spend
For any wasteful selfish end.
They are a trust that I must hold
As sacred. All the world's bright gold
Belongs to Him, and in my spending

I must repay His gracious lending.
God put His love within my heart,
A love I ever must impart
To a world in desperate need of care.
All things God gave me I must share.
This is the stewardship of living;
A spontaneous and a joyous giving.
—Grace Noll Crowell

Then we must have a big wide wonderful step of forgiveness. We must be willing to forgive those who "Tresspass against us." We must be willing to ask forgiveness for our own shortcomings and failures.

God has His own secret stairway into every heart, but we must keep the steps swept clean and polished with loving care.

4

The Higher Step

"Ye have heard that it has been said, Thou shalt love thy neighbor, and hate thine enemy. But I say unto you, Love your enemies, bless them that curse you, do good to them that hate you, and pray for them which despitefully use you." — Matthew 5:43-44

The morning had been hot and tiring. Part of the workers for the Vacation Bible School had not bothered to come. Now we wanted to close the day by taking pictures of the children in the school. Standing in the sun, feeling freckles popping out by the dozens, I was a bit impatient. The photographer was trying his best but he was having a hard time arranging the children.

"Will some of you please take the higher steps?" he asked the children.

Immediately there was a scramble to fill the highest step in front of the church. Soon the pictures were made and we were going home to our cool houses to rest from the work of the morning.

All afternoon the thought of some workers not bothering to come upset me. As I studied Matthew 5 for the next day's lesson I suddenly smiled.

23

"Why, Jesus was trying to teach the people to take the higher steps, in this chapter!" I exclaimed.

"But I say unto you, love your enemies." He expects us to take a higher step in applying the principle of love. I had not been working in the Bible School for my fellow workers. I had been working for the children and my Heavenly Father. They had certainly been present.

An old adage goes: "It costs more to avenge an ill than it does to bear one."

How many of Christ's followers have failed to catch the meaning of this principle. We love the lovable and attractive but we never bestow the gift of love upon the unlovely, the downtrodden, the outcast.

A young woman school teacher could not find a job in the town where she lived. Finally she was offered a place teaching the retarded children.

"Oh I just can't do it!" she told her friends. But because she so desperately needed to work she accepted the position.

In a few months she had learned to love the children and was studying ways to improve herself as a teacher. She stepped upon the higher step and learned to love those who were helpless.

Go up to the higher step. Do not be like so many modern day Christians who say, "Lord, I will serve you in all the ways I can, but please don't ask me to love the person who said ugly things about me."

"Surely you do not want me to love that person who said mean things, who is two-faced, stabbing me in the back when I am not present?"

Yes, God wants us to take a higher step. Jesus loved the world enough to give His life for those who abused Him.

We must try to see people through the eyes of Christian love. What would that person, who is evil and mean, be if they knew and trusted Christ.

A minister's wife was telling me about a very attractive

young lady in her town. "She leads the other young people astray. I covet her for the Lord."

Can you see someone evil and sinful and step up on a higher step by trying to win them for the Lord?

'Tis true, sometimes people mistreat us. Can we like true Christians step higher. Christ prayed on the cross, "Father forgive them." Can we pray for our enemies?

Forgiveness is a very high step. There must be no limit to our forgiveness. One of the disciples asked Christ if he should forgive his brother seven times. To this Jesus replied "until seventy times seven."

We must forgive even before those who offend us ask forgiveness. Someone has wisely said: "A true Christian must have a package of forgiveness, wrapped in love, tied with the bow of friendship, and offered in grace and humility."

Two men, members of the same church, became angry with each other. One of the men went to the pastor and told him the ugly story.

"When will you set things right?" the pastor asked him.

"What do you mean?" the man was startled. "He is the one in the wrong."

The pastor opened his Bible and read Matthew the fifth chapter and twenty-third verse.

"Therefore, if thou bring thy gift to the altar, and there rememberest that thy brother hath ought against thee; leave there thy gift and go thy way; first be reconciled to thy brother, and then come and offer thy gift."

After much prayer and reading of the Scriptures the man went to his enemy and asked him to be friends. Both men rededicated their lives to Christ. The whole church became revived. The men took the higher step by putting strife out of their lives and hearts.

If Christ had died only for the worthy ones, He would not have died at all, for "All have sinned."

If Christ had served only those who were grateful, and thanked him, He would have reduced His healing 90 per cent. There were ten lepers healed, but only one bothered to thank Him. Take the higher step — do not expect returns for each kind deed you do.

If Christ had fed only His friends, very few of the five thousand would have been fed.

Take the higher step. Look at people through the eyes of our Saviour.

Take the higher step. Ask, "Who can I make happy?" not, "Who will make me happy?"

I picked up the following poem in a cafeteria one day:

> Fully half the joy of living
> Is the joy of joyful giving . . .
> The other half is gratitude,
> Without stint or latitude.
>
> Then let's be thankful we're alive
> Can work, and laugh, and love and strive
> To make another life worth-while
> By glad'ning hearts that need our smile.

5

Joy Cometh in the Morning

"For his anger endureth but for a moment; in his favor is life: weeping may endure for a night, but joy cometh in the morning." — Psalm 30:5

Many people today suffer from earthly sorrows, physical pains, and the cares of this world. For the Christians there will come a day when all sorrow and pain will end. Joy for them will come when they meet the Saviour.

When World War I ended, I was just a small child in the first grade. The word reached Fort Worth, Texas, about three o'clock in the morning. The first thing I remember was waking up to hear noise. People were shouting, whistles were blowing, bells were ringing, somewhere a band could be heard faintly playing. Noise of every kind could be heard. We had no radios or televisions to tell us the good news, but we heard it just the same.

The boy next door was beating on a dishpan, so I ran into my mother's kitchen and found a tin pan. I began to beat my pan with a spoon. My mother was laughing and crying at the same time. Everyone in the city seemed to be happy. What a joyous morning that was. The war was over!

When World War II ended, I was a mother with three

children. My husband was just home after spending two years on the front lines in Europe. In our small town of two thousand people, we heard the news about mid-morning. Cars honked, someone rang the church bell, and the whistle at the mill blew. People ran into the streets calling out: "The war is over!" We had something to be happy about.

Think of the joy we will know on the resurrection morning. The war between Heaven and hell will be ended. The war between good and evil will cease. The Lord will descend from heaven with a shout, the trumpet of God will sound, the graves will burst open. The dead will arise.

There will be joy unheard of that glorious morning.

This will be a morning of victory — victory over the grave. The grave has robbed everyone of someone he knew and loved. There will be no more death. There will be no more pain and sorrow. It will be a morning of joy.

It will be a morning of victory over sin. Sin has brought only bad things to this earth. Sin causes sickness, shame, trouble. Sin causes wars and rumors of wars. Sin causes little children to have to go hungry, sin causes homes to be broken. Sin only leads down a dark path of night.

When sin is judged, then comes the morning. The morning for which all mornings were made. The morning of joy for the redeemed children of God.

When man fell in the garden, the night of sin started. Man was cast out of the presence of Heaven's light. Then many years later the day star appeared, our Lord Jesus Christ.

When the great morning of joy comes, all the saints will be gathered home.

A missionary friend of mine told me of her homecoming during World War II. She and another missionary had been in a Japanese prison camp on the Philippine Islands. They had suffered from hunger, loneliness, and fear. When the American troops liberated them, they were put aboard a ship bound for home. One night the captain told them they would dock early next morning in San Francisco. They were almost too excited to sleep. They were at the rail bright and early next morning. The fact that they had no clothes, no money, their mission field left behind, all was forgotten at the sight of all the people waiting on shore. As they watched, and knew in a few moments they would be greeting their loved ones again, the joy and safety of home would be realized, the wonder of it was just too much. Suddenly one of the girls became hysterical and started screaming. The ship's doctor had to be called and she was given medicine to calm her overwrought nerves.

> Oh the joy of gathering home
> Never more in sin to roam.

That joyous resurrection morning will be a morning of reunions with loved ones. We do not know how things will be, but we do know our Lord has gone to prepare for our coming.

There will be rewards for faithfulness. There will be worshiping and praise. "Every knee shall bow."

> Hail to the brightness of Zion's glad morning!
> Joy to the lands that in darkness have lain!
> Hushed be the accents of sorrow and mourning
> Zion in triumph begins her glad reign.
> —Thomas Hastings

6

Wealth of Friendship

"Greater love hath no man than this, that a man lay down his life for his friends. Ye are my friends, if ye do whatsoever I command you. Henceforth I call you not servants; for the servant knoweth not what his lord doeth: but I have called you friends; for all things that I have heard of my Father I have made known unto you."
                                                                — *John 15:13-15*

Someone has beautifully said:

> It is a good thing to be rich,
> And a good thing to be strong,
> But it is a better thing
> To be loved by many friends.

How wonderful it must have been for the ones close to Jesus to be called His friends! Today we can also count Jesus as our friend if we have given Him our life.

Too often we treat our friends as if they were a heating pad or an electric blanket, keeping them all tucked away until a cold night of trouble or sickness comes. Then we rush to get their aid and the warmth of their love to sustain us.

WEALTH OF FRIENDSHIP

A philosopher long ago said: "A man is rich if he possesses one true friend."

It is easy to have a host of friends to laugh with us, friends who enjoy our hospitality and our food; but friends who stand by us in the time of adversity are not so easy to find.

Some people are like the honey bee. They sip the nectar of your friendship for a short time, then flit away to flowering pastures. It is nice to keep all our friends, but we should never do so at the expense of our Christian principles.

The best and first friend anyone should have is, of course, our Lord and Saviour Jesus Christ. He is the friend who "sticketh closer than a brother.'" He is a friend whom we should endeavor to introduce to all our other friends. He is a friend we should ever seek to know better.

A deacon in a church once told me of his conversion. He was a wild boy and gave his widowed mother lots of trouble. With a friend he ran away from home. The boys were following a railroad track. When they were about half way across a long bridge the whistle of a train sounded. The boys became frightened. The other side looked too far away. They climbed down and hung to the bridge timbers. In a matter of seconds the train was roaring over their heads. As they hung there in great danger the boy suddenly realized his mother was a true friend and loved him. He began to pray and ask God to let him get home again. He said it seemed to him that, after he prayed and asked forgiveness for his wild wicked ways, a great strength came to his arms and hands. He was able to hold on until the roaring monster overhead was gone. When he reached home again, he went to the church and confessed his sins. Talking with the pastor later he discovered that his mother had been in the pastor's study asking the pastor to pray for her son at the very time he was in such great danger on the trestle.

One of the most important friends we have in this life is our chosen life companion. This friend should be selected with the greatest of care. Many homes are broken because a man and a woman have never really become friends. Lovers sometimes tire of each other, sex attractions often grow stale; but if a couple has a deep and abiding respect and friendship for each other they can build a home together.

How often we carelessly make the statement, "Oh, she is my friend, she will understand." We should always treat our friends with consideration, even if we do feel they will overlook our shortcomings. We need to let our friends know we love them and respect their wishes.

Sometimes a kind word or deed from a friend helps us to keep going when we want to quit. One Sunday I felt as if I were just wasting my time trying to teach a ladies' Sunday School class. They seemed not to care that I had spent long hours in preparation and visitation. There were other things I could be doing with my time! My family would like some of the attention I spent on my class.

After class that Sunday morning one of the class members handed me a folded sheet of paper. I did not get time to read it until after church. On the paper was a poem she had written just for me. It has been an inspiration and blessing to me many times since.

TO MY TEACHER

We know the ones who have acclaim,
In print, publicity and fame,
But sometimes there is a gentle heart,
Who takes an even greater part,
And by the thought, the word, the deed,
Fills in a void when there is need.

Her name is not in glowing print,
Nor listed there the time she spent,
In visiting with a lonely soul,
To help to make the sufferer whole.

Who with her husband comes by night,
To those bereaved who ask respite,
And comfort in the living word,
Consolence in the Scripture heard.

WEALTH OF FRIENDSHIP

> Yet often no attention's paid,
> To all the time she read and prayed,
> That we might have the living proof,
> Of all God's wonder and His truth.
> 'Tis with a grateful heart I say,
> God bless you, dear, on your birthday.
> Your Pupil
Frances Green

Do you wonder that as I read this tribute all my cares seemed to vanish away!

If all pupils could know how much their teachers long for just a word of encouragement, I believe they would take the time to say more.

In large churches where it is an impossibility for the pastor to visit each member often, if at all, the teachers fill a very important place in keeping close contact with the members.

We can never know how near a friend is to the breaking point. Maybe just a kind deed or word from us might mean the difference. It is not hard to tell people how much you appreciate them if you make it a practice and habit to do so.

We are free in America to choose our friends. We are free to argue with them, to try to change their opinions, to tell them our beliefs. We do not have to wonder if they are enemies seeking to catch us saying the wrong thing against our Government.

Although you might live in a very humble cottage, or in the finest of mansions, you can be wealthy with friends. You can know the friend of all people. You can tell others about Him.

Thanksgiving

"Give thanks always for all things unto God."
— *Ephesian 5:20*

One time I was asked to bring a Thanksgiving devotional to a group of women. I knew most of the ladies who would be present were very wealthy. My devotional was a comparison of the modern day conveniences with those of our grandmothers and grandfathers. It was a gentle hint that we should be so thankful we live in this day and age. When I finished the ladies all began to laugh and chatter about how they had managed when they were younger and automatic washers were something unheard of.

We so often take our blessings for granted. One of the women told of coming as a pioneer to the state of New Mexico. She and her husband and baby son traveled in a covered wagon. The weather turned so cold a bucket of water hanging on the bow of the wagon froze. She told how they almost starved trying to make a crop without rain. When all those women were through talking and sharing experiences, they realized they had a great many things for which to be thankful.

THANKSGIVING

THANKS

Did I forget to thank thee, Lord,
For things that may seem small . . .
A flower by the wayside path,
A wild bird's lonely call;

For all the daily happenings
That we call commonplace,
For sunrise and for sunset glow,
My neighbor's smiling face?

Since life is made of little things,
Oh, let me not forget
To count my smallest blessings all,
Before the sun is set.

I thank thee, Lord, for every one
Who adds a note of cheer,
And for the blessings multiplied
To me from year to year.
—J. T. Bolding

"Many, O Lord my God, are thy wonderful works which thou hast done . . . if I would declare and speak of them, they are more than can be numbered" (Psalm 40:5).

Have you ever been in the hospital and you could not have a drink of water? For a few hours you burned with fever, but no water were you allowed. In your thirsty condition you could picture tall glasses of cold water. You could imagine springs of water flowing down the mountain side. You felt little relief when the nurse placed a damp cloth on your feverish lips. Yet, do we ever just pause at the sink and thank our Father for water to drink?

Today we find so many people in the hospitals who can only breathe with the aid of oxygen. Do you take the air you breathe for granted? Step out into the open air and take a good deep breath. Then thank God for pure air to breathe. This book could not contain a list of all the everyday little things for which we forget to give thanks.

Then there are so many larger things for which we should give thanks.

I have a very dear friend who, when a church group needs a meeting place, is always saying,

"You are welcome to meet at my house."

One day I asked her why she was so generous with her home.

"Because I have not always had a lovely home to offer to my friends."

Then she told me the following story.

When she was a young school teacher, she met and married a railroad worker. He was foreman over a group of men who traveled from town to town repairing tracks and putting in new ones. The men and their families lived in boxcar houses. She lived in her boxcar home for several years. Her two little boys had no yard to play in, and often no other children to play with. Whenever they pulled onto the sidetrack in a new town, she found her way to the local church. She went to all the services and tried to make friends. She found people would start to act coolly to her when she told them where she lived. She became "one of those railroaders' wives."

So she started asking the Mission Society women to come to her boxcar home for meetings. They went out of curiosity but they found a place clean and neat. Her prayer through those years was for a house like other women had. When the years passed and her husband advanced in his work he was given a permanent station. She has tried to show her thankfulness by being very generous with her home.

Often we take our lovely, comfortable homes for granted. We take our families as just a matter of course. If we but stop and think we realize there are many people in the world who would give a great deal just to belong to someone — little children living in groups, children left without parents because of war.

As Americans we should be so thankful for space. Many times in recent years I have read stories of crowded conditions in countries whose cities were destroyed by war. Families sleep on sidewalks, or make shelters on top of buildings.

THANKSGIVING

There are places in our great western United States where one can drive for miles and not see a house.

We should be thankful for the ability to share. Last Christmas our phone rang. A mother of nine children was calling. She asked, not for turkey and fancy food, just something to fill her hungry children's stomachs. As we filled a box of groceries from our pantry, we thanked God we were the ones who could share in place of being the ones in need.

OUR THANKS TO THEE

There is so much we have in life
For which we cannot pay,
The things we take for granted
In our journey day by day.

From early in the morning
Until the day is done,
We ought to count our blessings
And name them one by one.

Health, peace, happiness;
Love of kin and friends;
Birds, trees, flowers, seas;
A list that never ends.

Summer, autumn, winter, spring,
Each brings something rare,
And we accept what comes our way
Without a thought or care.

We really ought to think a bit
Of what we have, and why.
There is so much belongs to us —
The stars, the moon, the sky;

The very air we breath each day,
And food upon the board;
And the only way we can ever pay —
"Our thanks to Thee, O Lord."
—Author unknown

Let us stop being careless and taking things for granted. Let's be grateful!

We can show our gratitude for the greatest of all blessings, our Lord, by telling others of His blessings.

8

Date with Destiny

"And who knoweth whether thou art come to the king-dom for such a time as this?" — Esther 4:14

God has given us this time and age in which to live. We had no choice about it. Yet we have a responsibility as to what we will do with our time and talents while living in this age.

> Life is a story in Volumes three,
> The past, the present, and yet-to-be.
> The first is finished and laid away
> The second we're reading day by day.
> The third and the last of volume three,
> Is locked from sight, God keeping the key.
> —Selected

So you have an hour, and that hour is, "Such a time as this."

Kernie Keegan, a worker among young people, wrote before his death the following: "You occupy a special place in God's purpose. No one else can fill it. Your will surrendered to God's infinite will makes you a part of the infinite. Eternity is yours now in Christ. Believe this and you will be a blessing."

DATE WITH DESTINY

This is our date with destiny; what do we find? This is our date with destiny, what will we do?

We find race tensions. Often we forget God created all men. More often we forget God created all men equal. We have but to read our daily news to know that many suffer because of their color or because of an unpopular religious creed. Each of us must search his own life. We must be honest with ourselves as we think of our day and our destiny. What stand will we take on world issues? Can we be true to the teachings of the Bible concerning others?

Our date with destiny comes in a day of many broken homes and wrong family relationships. Can we make our own homes examples of Christian love and fellowship? Everyone can exert some influence over his own home. If our homes, the very foundation of our society, fail, then soon our government will fail.

Our day of destiny finds among many of our leaders in church and in government, a lowering of ideals and standards.

At times we wonder just how Christian are our Christian leaders. Just how interested in the welfare of our nation are our leaders.

> This is our date with destiny.
> This is our hour to spend.
> Now is the time to get ready
> For eternity coming and without end.

Eternity will be richer because of your resolves today. Now is the time to determine the degree of conquest Christ has over your will.

> I have only just a minute,
> Only sixty seconds in it,
> Forced upon me,
> Can't refuse it,
>
> Didn't seek it,
> Didn't choose it,
> But it's up to me to use it.
> I must suffer if I lose it,

PLEASE GIVE A DEVOTION

Give account if I abuse it;
Just a tiny little minute —
But eternity is in it.
                    —Author unknown

Our date with destiny and what do we bring to it? We bring our home training. Most of us have had the joy and advantages of Christian homes, the security and happiness of Christian parents. We have known freedom of worship all our life time. Are we taking these blessings for granted? Will we work to see that other people in other lands know the same freedom? Will we preserve for our children the privileges given to us?

Historians explain the past; economists explain the future; only the present is confusing. The present is our day, our hour.

We have the influence of great men and women who have lived before us. If we read and study, their influence will help us in our decisions. Above all we should let Christ influence us.

In speaking to Esther, Mordecai said: "For if thou altogether holdest thy peace at this time thou and thy father's house shall be destroyed."

Are we holding our peace and letting those around us be destroyed for lack of knowledge? Do we have no time in our hour of destiny to speak for God?

We must live in this age; we cannot choose another. Yet what an age in which to live!

We live in a time of challenges. We have seen undreamed of feats accomplished — marvelous advances in science, in medicine and in the modes of travel. We talk glibly about space, about men going around the world in short periods of time. We have a responsibility to our day and age.

How well I remember, as a little girl, listening to the radio, and wishing so much I could see the performers. Now we have television. We have ways of transmitting sound and pictures unheard of just a few years back.

DATE WITH DESTINY

A poet has expressed the wonder of our day of destiny as follows:

TODAY

To be alive in such an age!
With every year a lightening page
Turned in the world's great wonder book
Whereon the leaning nations look.

When men speak strong for brotherhood,
For peace and universal good,
When miracles are everywhere
And every inch of common air

Throbs a tremendous prophecy
Of greater marvels yet to be.
Oh thrilling age,
Oh willing age!

Seeing beneath the world's unrest
Creation's huge untiring quest.

Your hour of destiny, what will you do with it?

9

What Do You See?

"Moreover the word of the Lord came unto me, saying, Jeremiah, what seest thou? And I said, I see a rod of an almond tree." — Jeremiah 1:11

One summer a family traveled from the flat dry plains of West Texas to the high Rocky Mountains of Colorado. As they drew near the mountains the children began to talk about what they would see when they reached the top of Pike's Peak. They saw many things of interest as they drove up the steep road — the sharp curves, the cars far below them, the people stalled because of overheated cars — but the uppermost thought in their minds was, "What will we see from the top?"

What elation for the little group when at last they parked the car and stood on top of the peak. They felt sorry for all the people back in their home town who could not see what they were seeing. They saw a city many miles away. They saw the little train bringing people to the top. They saw a wrecked airplane on a mountainside. They saw snow, and a rain cloud raining over a spot far across the peaks. The children were well pleased with their trip. They took turns looking through field glasses to find new things to see.

WHAT DO YOU SEE?

Next day they came to the top of another mountain. A sign read "The Great Divide." Getting out of the car they looked all about. All they could see was trees and snow. The forest completely obstructed the view of far off things. They were disappointed and soon asked to drive on to other sights.

Jeremiah saw a rod of an almond tree, a symbol of the Judgment of God on His people. In Zechariah 4:1-7, the prophet was asked what he saw. He saw things symbolizing the spirit of God.

When we look out on our world today, what do we see? Like the little family on Pipe's Peak we can see far and wide. We have newspapers, radios, television, magazines, books, to help us see our world.

Yet with all the modern media of news, we see what we want to see. When we look at our world, do we see the thorn and the thistle, the curse of the earth? Do we see wars and rumors of wars? We can look through dark glasses and see only sadness and sin, trouble and sorrow.

What do we see? We must look for the beauty of the earth. God wrought beauty in the flowers, in the fruit of the ground, in all the loveliness of nature. Take a trip to any part of our world and you will see things only a great creator could make. Go out into your own garden and you will see the wonder of growing things. There are many good things to see if we look for the good. In the joy of fellowship with dear friends and precious families we can see the hand of God.

Take a look through the written Word of God and what do we see?

There is Balaam on top of Mt. Pisgah, meeting God and receiving a blessing for Jacob. Stand with Moses on top of the mountain and we can see over into the promised land. Stand with Elisha in Samaria and see the great hosts of God protecting His own. Stand with Elijah on Mount Carmel and see the fire of God descend to lick up the sacrifice of God.

Look around our world, what do you see? See the churches over our nation. See the Christian armies as they march on, at home and on the mission fields. Stand with Peter, James, and John on the Mount of Transfiguration and see our conquering glorified Christ.

> What do you see?
> Look at our world.
> Do you see the need
> For men to be told
> Of Jesus our saviour?
> Or is your heart cold?
> Are you only seeking
> For silver and gold?

Look at your life and find an answer today. Mable Niedermeyer has written the following poem:

FINDING GOD

> I helped a little child to see
> That God had made a willow tree,
> And He became more real to me.
> I tried to lead a child through play
> To grow more Christlike every day,
> And as we bowed in worship there
> I felt anew God's loving care.
> Lord, keep us ever quick to see
> By guiding children we find thee.

10

Time

"To every thing there is a season, and a time to every purpose under heaven: a time to be born, and a time to die; a time to plant and a time to pluck up that which is planted. . . . A time to love, a time to hate; a time of war and a time of peace." — Ecclesiastes 3:1, 2, 8

> Sixty seconds make a minute
> How much good can I do with it?
> Sixty minutes make an hour,
> I'll do all that's in my power.
> Twenty-four hours make a day
> Time for work and time for play
> —From an old school reader

Time is among our most valuable possessions. Every person has twenty-four hours each day he lives. Some make use of time and some waste it away.

At best the time of our present lives is short. It can only be from the cradle to the grave. Only God knows how long that will be. I like a small verse I clipped from a paper.

GOD'S MINUTE

> I have only just a minute,
> Only sixty seconds in it,
> Forced upon me, can't refuse it,
> Didn't seek it, didn't choose it,

But it's up to me to use it,
I must suffer if I lose it,
Give account if I abuse it,
But Eternity is in it.
—Author Unknown

Often we live as if time were ours to spend as we please. When we realize it never waits but is continually passing, it is often too late. Time can never be recalled.

One afternoon a small boy failed to return home from school. The mother became alarmed but waited for the return of the father from work. When the father had exhausted himself looking over the neighborhood he called the child's teacher.

"He had to stay in after school," the teacher told the distracted father. "He made very poor grades this month."

"He asked me to help him with his arithmetic, but I was so busy," the father said.

Two days later when the body of the child was found, the sad story was completed. Rather than face taking home poor grades he had gone out into the woods and frozen to death.

"Oh if I had just taken time to help my boy!" the father said over and over, but he could not call back the past.

Some of the saddest words to be heard on this earth are, "Too Late."

Time is so precious we should give careful consideration to its proper use.

Jesus said in Matthew 6:33, "Seek ye first the kingdom of God, and his righteousness; and all these things shall be added unto you."

Do we have time not to put first things first? The following poem tells in poetic form the type of lives we live.

NO TIME FOR GOD?

You've time to build houses, and in them to dwell
And time to do business — to buy and to sell
But none for repentance, or deep earnest prayer,
To seek your salvation you've no time to spare.

TIME

You've time for earth's pleasures, for frolic, for fun
For her glittering treasures how quickly you run,
But care not to seek the fair mansions above,
The favor of God or the gift of His love.

You've time to take voyages over the sea,
And time to take in the gay world's jubilee;
But soon your bright hopes will be lost in the gloom
Of the cold, dark river of death, and the tomb.

You've time to resort to woods, mountain and glen,
And time to gain knowledge from books and of men,
Yet no time to search for the wisdom of God?
But what of your soul when you're under the sod?

For time will not linger when helpless you lie;
Staring death in the face you will take time to die!
Then, what of the judgment? Pause, think, I implore!
For time soon will be lost on eternity's shore.

—Author Unknown

In I Corinthians 7:29 Paul said, "But this I say, brethren, the time is short."

The first thing for all to do is to seek the Lord. "Seek ye the Lord while he may be found."

The second thing is to serve the Lord. All other things will then fall into their rightful places.

A young minister once wanted very much to make a trip to attend a convention. He did not have the money and his church was too poor to send him. He felt discouraged and alone; all the other ministers in his district were going.

At noon the day before time to go, his wife placed the morning mail beside his plate.

When he opened the first letter a check fluttered out and fell to the floor. The check was for an amount large enough to pay the convention expenses. The accompanying letter read: "A gift for you because you took time to teach me the right way when I was confused."

The right use of his time paid off, when he expected it least, and needed it most.

Someone has said, "Yesterday is a canceled check, tomorrow is a check uncashed, today is cash in the pocket."

Make use of your precious gift of time.

11

The Grace of Gratitude

"Many, O Lord my God, are thy wonderful works which thou hast done, and thy thoughts which are to us-ward: They cannot be reckoned up in order unto thee: if I would declare and speak of them, they are more than can be numbered." — Psalm 40:5

Do we forget to show gratitude to God for all His wonderful blessings? A friend one day told me she felt her life was so unhappy she had nothing for which to be grateful.

One time I spent a few days in the hospital. After the operation was over I could not have a drink of water. How I thirsted for a cool glass of water! Even the damp cloth placed on my lips helped a little. Have you ever been away from home and longed for a drink of your hometown water?

How grateful we should be for water to drink, for air to breathe, for homes, children, friends, church, freedom. God has given us so many things for which we should thank Him. Yet we take the little things for granted. Watch someone under an oxygen tent in a hospital; then you will know how thankful you should be for the ability to breathe.

We often fail to show gratitude to our friends when they go to the trouble of preparing gifts or meals for us.

THE GRACE OF GRATITUDE

Children are sometimes ungrateful to parents for the many sacrifices they make in order to send them to school. A kind family in our church adopted a small child. They made her understand she would always live with them.

In the Sunday School class the teacher asked if any child would like to say a prayer of thanks. The adopted child prayed: "Thank you God for a mommie and daddy who are not going to leave me."

A friend who spends her time at home with an afflicted child, giving private music lessons to help support her family shows a grace of gratitude when she always ends her prayers with the words: "Help me dear Father to show gratitude for all your many blessings."

We too often just take our comfortable, lovely homes for granted. How grateful we should be for Christian homes! They tell us the great city of Hong Kong is so crowded people live on the roof tops.

How grateful we should be for the privilege of sharing! Often we read in the papers of some person being found dead of starvation, yet on their person or hidden in their room would be thousands of dollars.

When my children were small we lived in a village. My husband was pastor of the church but we received only enough salary to keep food on the table and our car in running condition. At Christmas time the wealthiest woman in the church came with big boxes of clothes and linens for our family. How proud we were of those nice gifts! She was grateful enough for her own good fortune to share with those in need.

> Oh God, make me thankful
> For every bird on wings.
> Give me the grace of gratitude
> For all life's little things.

12

Invisible Price Tags

"For the wages of sin is death; but the gift of God is eternal life through Jesus Christ our Lord."
— *Romans 6:23*

"Isn't it fun to go shopping?"

Even just wandering through the dime store is interesting. All the new gadgets one can find to spend money on!

In our town we have a so-called "Dollar-day." Now that is a place to be very careful. If I am not on my toes I go home with something I do not need or that is not worth the price I paid.

I have now adopted a slogan: "Nothing is a bargain unless you really need it."

I once knew a lady who attended all the sales and bought anything she thought a bargain; then she tried to re-sell her so-called bargains to her friends and children.

All shoppers are alike in one respect; they may be young, they may be old, beautiful or ugly, but their fingers just naturally reach for the price tag. They look at the price tag and ask themselves a question.

"Can I afford this? Is it worth the price?"

An insurance salesman I once knew went into a large store

in Dallas, Texas. He found a very attractive sport coat. He could not see the price tag and was too proud to ask. He bought the coat, had it charged and went out of the store happy. When the bill came the price was $185. He was astonished but had worn the coat and could not return it.

If we are concerned about the price of material things — such as clothes, food, homes, and have in mind approximate prices which we will not go over, what about the spiritual things.

There are many, many things in life with invisible price tags. You may long to have a musical instrument and play in the band. My own son once worked all summer in order to buy a clarinet. We felt the price was too high. He went to school proud and happy with his beautiful horn. The next year he was given a scholarship in college if he would play his horn in the band. So his instrument was worth the sacrifice after all.

Young people standing on the threshold of life need to ask themselves, "What is the invisible price tag?"

A young man pays a small amount for a drink of liquor. Maybe in a few years he cannot keep from drinking constantly. He did not see the price tag of a ruined career, and maybe a broken home.

A very promising young high school senior went on an outing with his class. Some of the couples began petting, one thing led to another, and for the moment that young man forgot the price of promiscuous lovemaking. In the fall when others were packing for college the brightest one in the class was being forced to marry. He did not care for the girl but he paid the price.

There are few bargains in life. One needs to remember that most successful people paid for their success in hard work and self-denial. Paderewski paid for his popularity as a musician by many years of practice. Dr. Mayo of Rochester, paid for his fame as a healer by a great amount of study.

Everything in life has a price tag, visible or invisible. The

51

prodigal son could not see the price he was going to pay. The rich young ruler thought the price of eternal life too high. Judas realized too late the price he paid for thirty pieces of silver.

Many girls pay too great a price for pretty clothes. Many boys and girls pay too much for popularity and surface friends. Learn now to search for the price at the present and in the future.

The cheapest thing in the world is a kind and loving word. Yet the value of a kind word on a life is hard to measure. Look for life's price tag and be prepared to make the best selections of how you will spend the time and talent alloted to you.

13

Hands of Christ

"*And he took the blind man by the hand, and put his hands upon him.*" — *Mark 8:23*

"*My times are in thy hand; deliver me from the hand of mine enemies, and from them that persecute me. Make thy face to shine upon thy servant: save me for thy mercies sake.*" — *Psalm 31:15, 16*

And as I pondered on His holy Word
The Spirit's light illumed my blinded eyes;
I knew the secret of the yielded life,
I saw self slain, and arose to realize
My times were in His hand and in His hand indeed.
My part was but to walk and faithful be,
Nor anxious when my strength was sorely tried,
For He was earnest of my eternity.
My times are in His hand. I know it now,
And O, the peace and confidence it brings!
And gratitude wells up within my soul
As closer to His heart my spirit clings.
A sinner lost but for His boundless love,
He cares for me though unclean and defiled;
Unfaithful and unworthy though I be,
My times are in His hands! Thank God I am His child!
                                        —Charles C. Kiser

The human hand is a wonderful part of the body. A great

actor can convey a message by the use of his hands. An artist can use his hands to wield a brush and paint a beautiful picture. A magician can entertain great audiences with the quickness of his hands. A surgeon can use his hands to help bring relief to suffering humanity. Many pages could be written about the use and wonder of the human hand. We should all be thankful for our hands.

People have been known to be born without hands. People have lost parts or all of their hands through accidents or diseases. There have been very clever and useful artificial hands made for use of such unfortunate people.

As you read the Gospels you will be astonished at the number of times Jesus laid His hands upon people who were in trouble. He is still just as ready to help people today if they will but place their faith in Him.

Jesus' hands were hands of blessing. We find he used his hands to bless others. How wonderful the lives of the little children must have been after he placed his hands upon them and blessed them! Mark 10:16 pictures Jesus blessing the children. Luke 24:50 gives a picture of His blessing the disciples. He lifted his hand in blessing as he ascended to the Father.

I am sure during the years Jesus lived with Joseph and Mary at the carpenter shop He worked with His hands.

UNDER CHRIST'S GUIDING HAND

I stood on the mountain top so high
And looked out over the land;
The flying birds way up in the sky;
They were made by His guiding hand.

The flowing rushing water below
Of the countless rivers winding their way,
The flowers growing as only they know,
Sleeping in winter; blooming in May.

The trees reaching up to the heavens above
Giving their shade to some passer-by;
With hearts so young and full of love
They flocked, the children, to play nearby.

HANDS OF CHRIST

All this came from One so great
He made each thing as only He can
Nothing on earth came by mere fate
God made it all; He even made man.

If He knows every feather of every bird
And every grain of the shifting sand
Then I know that just as it says in His Word
I too, am under Christ's Guiding Hand.
                              —Joy Souther

Have a look at the hands of your friends and neighbors; they tell a story. It is easy to tell the hands of a working man; they are rough and often calloused. Some are knotted with disease and age. Some hands are soft and white, never being used for useful deeds. Some hands are lifted in prayer each day. Some hands are used to soothe a fevered brow.

Whatever our talents, we have a duty to use our hands as Christ used His, to bless the world.

I have two hands which I must use
If I would like my Master be,
To heal the sick, and help the blind,
To show my Saviour to all mankind.

I have two hands, O use them Lord,
To help blind men to see
The hope of life eternal
A better world yet to be.

Whatever your station in life there is a task for you to accomplish. In our town there is a free clinic for sick babies. Many women have found as they worked there, a satisfaction from the use of their hands they had never known before. Two faithful doctors give up their lunch hour several days each week to care for those poor children. Many of the mothers bring children to the clinic and cannot speak English to tell the symptoms.

In every place where there are people, there are tasks to be accomplished by the use of dedicated Christian hands.

What a host of hands there would be if all the hands of faithful teachers of God's Word were suddenly held up toward heaven!

When you find a task you cannot accomplish alone, and that is often, always remember He will help with hands which are all-powerful. So how can we fail if our hands are dedicated to God's use?

14

Joy of Service

"And whosoever of you will be the chiefest, shall be servant of all." — Mark 10:44

The people who live on and on in history are the people who have served others the most. Look at Christ and His great kingdom. Did He in any way try to serve himself? He lived and died for others.

Someone has said God did not pronounce a curse on man when He told him he would have to work for a livelihood. There is a joy and a contentment about being able to go out and work each day. The person who lives for himself alone and never serves others in any way, is a miserable person indeed.

I lived in a small town one time when a great tragedy occurred. Two large healthy men lived in their mother's home. Each month she received a pension check. The two men never worked but they took the mother's check and spent it. The check was not enough for so many people to live on. In place of going out to get jobs they began to fight over the pension check. One day the older of the two grabbed the check from the postman and started to run toward town. The brother jumped in his car and ran his brother down.

He ran over him then backed up and ran over him again. The poor man's wife ran out to try to help her husband. The man in the car ran over her and so he was able to have his mother's pension check to pay on the funeral expenses of the two he had killed.

Service to others does not bring the sorrow that greed and selfishness does.

The joy of service comes from knowing we have helped others — that we have accomplished some task.

We should want to live a life of service because we were bought with a price. To serve our Master should be our chief aim in life.

Christ is worthy of our service.

The person who works to fill his place in the world gets self-respect. Many young men when faced with serving their country have quoted the following lines:

> I have to live with myself,
> And so
> I want to be fit for myself
> To know.

Self-respect in itself will make a person more content with life.

LIFE'S STEWARDSHIP

> If I have strength, I owe the service of the strong;
> If melody I have, I owe the world a song;
> If I can stand when all around me folk are falling,
> If I can run with speed when needy hearts are calling,
> And if my torch can light the dark of any night,
> Then I must pay the debt I owe with living light.
> —Charles Coke Woods

There is a joy in service found in fellowship. There is a joy in being with others who work also. The joy of fellowship is proved by so many different types of conventions. Even the coin-collectors have a convention.

JOY OF SERVICE

Service to others brings the reward of faith — faith to believe the best of those with whom we work — faith to believe in the basic fair play of those with whom we work and serve.

> No matter what others are doing, my friend,
> Or what they are leaving undone,
> God's counting on you to keep on with the job
> 'Til the very last battle is won.
>
> He's counting on you to be faithful;
> He's counting on you to be true.
> Yes, others may work, or others may shirk,
> But remember — God is counting on you.
> —Author Unknown

There are many kinds of service. There is the service of filling a useful place in the community by holding down a regular job. Then there is the service to the boss who employes us. He has a right to expect our best.

We are often called upon to give a sacrificial service in our home. Just remember how lonely life would be if we had no homes, no loved ones to care for and work for.

Then last and very important is the joy of service, a surrendered service, in our church.

One of the happiest people I have ever known, was a young man who wanted to serve his church. He was not well educated but he knew how to use his hands. One of the departments in his church needed painting. He was not a painter by trade but he bought some paint, asked a group of teen-age boys to help and they went to work. One time, after several years, I asked him how many coats of paint that intermediate department had.

"Well, I don't mind buying the paint, and if it will help the young ones to have an interest, I just call them together and we start in."

From that young man's work, a great number of boys have been led to live cleaner, better lives.

59

PLEASE GIVE A DEVOTION

One life is all too brief
In which to do the things we ought;
And we may come to grief
If in neglect's tight web we're caught.

—J. T. Bolding

There are many different motives for service. The Apostle Paul said in II Corinthians 5:12, "The love of Christ constraineth me."

We work for many different reasons. A man works hard for his family because he loves them. Christians work hard for their churches because they love the Lord.

For the person who goes through life doing his best in the place he has to serve, there is always the joy of rest — the peace that comes at the close of the day. For the Christians there is the joy of eternity's glory.

Lord, when I am weary with toiling,
And burdensome seem Thy commands;
Lord, show me Thy Hands.
Thy nail-pierced Hands, Thy Cross-torn Hands;
My Saviour, show me Thy Hands.
O God, dare I show Thee my hands?

—Author Unknown

15

Whither Bound?

"And he said, Hagar, Sarai's maid, whence camest thou? and whither wilt thou go? And she said, I flee from the face of my mistress Sarai." — Genesis 16:8

As we stand on the threshold of a new year, we think of the fact that we are moving into the future. As we hold the lighted torch of a new year in our hand, it is as though someone is saying to each of us, "Whither wilt thou go?"

Each year past has brought great changes in our world. Men who grew up never going past the county seat are now sending their sons and daughters on trips around the world. Are we sending with them a firm, secure faith in God?

Standing today looking to the future we wonder about our world, "Whither goest thou?" Space age has brought with it new challenges, new responsibilities. If someone asked each of us, "What are you going to do with this new year — with this new age, what do you contemplate?" will we listlessly say, "Oh nothing?"

Life is not like that. There are things to be accomplished in every age, in every year; and the Christian must work while there is time.

There is a future. We are promised one by our creator.

He breathed into us the breath of life. He promised if we believe on Him we shall never die. So we have a future to look forward to. There are many in the world today who do not know our God; they see no hope of a future. Ask them the question, "Whither goest thou?" They would give the sad answer, "We do not know."

It is true the world picture looks dark today. There is unrest on every hand. There are hungry people in many lands. There is ignorance and strife; but for the children of God there is a bright promise of tomorrow — the promise of the coming of the Kingdom, of victory over the world.

Each Christian, each church, has a part in the future of God's Kingdom. We are commanded: "Seek ye first the kingdom of God."

If you were living when the last nation-wide census was taken, you became a dot on a census tape. The government has machines to tabulate the people. Machines are wonderful in the things they can do but a child of God is not just a mere dot on a census tape. A child of God is someone going somewhere.

> I am a stranger here, within a
>   foreign land;
> My home is far away, upon a
>   golden strand;
> Ambassador to be of realms
>   beyond the sea,
> I'm here on business for my King.
>   —E. T. Cassel

Whither are ye bound? Christians are bound for home, a heavenly home. There is much to be accomplished for some before they reach that home.

It seems that man is anxious to reach the moon. Man may even reach the moon before this is printed. Christians have a responsibility to the masses over the world. They cry for help, for light to show the way.

One night my husband was called to a hotel room. A salesman there wanted someone to show him the way of salvation. He had the desire so much that he had called a stranger to come and explain the way. So many are lost! They do not know where they are going and they do not ask the way. We must go and tell them without being asked. Walt Huntley has stated it well in a verse.

> It's not the moon we need to reach,
>   It's God who put it there;
> The one who went to Calvary,
>   A rugged cross to bear:
> For sins of men with wicked hearts,
>   He died one afternoon;
> With faith in Him you'll have no fear
>   If man should reach the moon.

Whither goest thou? You are a part of something very big; so you have a big responsibility. What will you do about it this new year?

THE NEW YEAR

> Come let us anew
> Our journey persue, —
> Roll round with the year,
> And never stand still till the Master appear;
> His adorable will
> Let us gladly fulfil,
> And our talents improve
> By the patience of hope and the labor of love.
>
> Our life is a dream;
> Our time as a stream,
> Glides swiftly away,
> And the fugitive moment refuses to stay:
> The arrow is flown;
> The moment is gone;
> The millennial year
> Rushes on to our view, and eternity's near.
>
> Oh that each, in the day
> Of His coming may say,
> "I have fought my way through;
> I have finished the work thou didst give me to do";
> Oh that each from His Lord
> May receive the glad word,
> "Well and faithfully done;
> Enter into my joy, and sit down by my throne."
>   —Charles Wesley

16

Visitation—"Go Ye!"

"Go ye therefore, and teach all nations, baptizing them in the name of the Father, and of the Son and of the Holy Ghost: Teaching them to observe all things whatsoever I have commanded you: and, lo, I am with you alway, even unto the end of the world."
— *Matthew 28:19, 20*

GO!

There's an art in visitation,
    As you'll hear some glibly say;
There's a knack to meeting people
    In a glad and blessed way.
But the Visitation talent
    In your life will never grow
Until with determination
    You resolve, get up, and GO!
— J. T. Bolding

Some years back a prominent denomination in the South adopted for their slogan, "When we go, they come." This was not so new as it might have seemed. When Christ was on earth he did not spend all his time in the Temple. He went out among the people, to select his helpers, to heal the sick, to teach, and to heal. Visitation was so important to our

VISITATION — "GO YE!"

Lord, he gave a command to his followers to "Go Ye." That command is still in effect today. The Christians who grow, are the ones who go out to tell others of Jesus.

Visitation is more than just going to visit in the home of some person who has not heard of Jesus. Visitation can be a way of life for a Christian. It is a way of going out to meet the world with a smiling face — with an air which says, "I have a formula for a better life. I would like to share it with you."

A very busy man had a caller in his office one day. The visitor said he would like to lease a piece of land. As they talked the visitor suddenly said, "I'm up here to see about my son. He is attending college."

The business man, a devout Christian, a worker with college students, immediately opened his ears.

"What church is your son attending?" he asked.

"Why, I don't know. He may not go at all." The visitor replied. "On Easter we go to one at home."

"You should go back out to the college and talk to your boy. He needs the guidance of a church." The business man made a note on his pad to see about the boy himself.

"Well," said the visitor, "I see you are too busy to listen to the troubles of my boy." With these words the worried father started out the door.

"Wait! said the business man, "I am never too busy to work for my Lord." He went over and gently closed the door. "Take a seat."

One hour later a happy new Christian left that office. He left to go find his son and tell him there was a better way of life.

The command to "Go Ye" still is in effect today, not just for those who have lots of time to spend, but to all who profess the name of Christ.

We must visit wherever we go with a smiling face and an enthusiastic spirit — to talk of My Church, My Pastor, with zeal and enthusiasm, and above all to tell of the glories of

My Saviour. Enthusiasm is contagious and we want to give it to others.

When a Christian rests he rusts. So a real Christian will want to go out and tell others of Christ.

Some people are always complaining. They complain about their lot in life; their blessings are not as wonderful as those of their friend and neighbor. Look at that person's life and more than likely you will see a person who does just enough to get by. Our world is filled with many people today who do not care to do a job well, just to get by and draw their pay.

There can be no end to the wages we draw when we follow faithfully Jesus' command to, "Go Ye." We have His promise, "Lo, I am with you always." If he is with us we know things will be the best for us.

If we are to be successful in carrying out our commission, we must be willing to spend time upon our knees praying. We go in vain unless the Holy Spirit guides our steps.

After we have spent time in prayer we must be willing to spend gasoline, cars, shoe leather, to follow where He leads us.

WHY?

It is just not convenient to tell FRIEND today
That we care for his soul in a real sort of way,
So we drift through today and await one that's fair,
And he goes on and on, knowing not that we care.
Yet we claim that we care as we come to the Lord
With our needs stacked high and requests by the cord;
But I wonder how we can explain to Him why
We don't share the "good news" as we watch lost men die.

17

Beauty Box

"Let the beauty of the Lord our God be upon us."
                                    — Psalm 90:17

There is an old Chinese Proverb which goes like this:

> If there is righteousness in the heart,
> There will be beauty in the character.
> If there is beauty in the character,
> There will be harmony in the home,
> If there is harmony in the home,
> There will be order in the nation,
> There will be peace in the world.

The whole world is interested in beauty today. We spend money to travel and see the beautiful things in the world. In some cities we have beauty schools, where people learn how to make the body more beautiful. We have charm schools where people learn how to be more beautiful in manners and dress. Have you ever thought of the place where we learn to be beautiful in spirit?

To have a beautiful spirit we must first of all have love. We should hold our love for others as we would a box of precious jewels. We might take as our motto part of the song "My Task."

To love someone more dearly ev'ry day,
To help a wandering child to find his way.
To ponder o'er a noble thought and pray
And smile when evening falls.
This is my task.

—Maude Louise Ray

Hold love as you would hold earth's dearest treasure. Make an extra effort to hold the love of family and friends. If you had a thousand friends you would not have one to spare. Love will win a battle when hate only kills and ruins.

If you would have a beautiful spirit, be good humored. There is virtue in good humor. In the Bible we have many verses on good humor. One even states "God loveth a cheerful giver." Another verse, Proverbs 15:13, reads, "A merry heart maketh a cheerful countenance."

Take for your motto, "Smile and the world smiles with you, cry and you cry alone."

When you feel you must complain, smile.
Do not care if things seem gray,
Soon there will come a brighter day.
You will find that it will pay, to smile.

To have a truly beautiful spirit learn not the art of nagging.

Nagging and bragging,
Are two silly things.
They make people unhappy
And cause only pains.
So never allow yourself to nag
And remember the world hates
Those who constantly brag.

Be content with your life. Paul said, "I have learned in whatsoever state I am to be content." How we dread to spend an hour in the company of a person who is filled with discontent. We leave them feeling depressed.

To be beautiful we must scatter seeds of kindness. They will spring up and grow along the paths we have traveled.

BEAUTY BOX

SEEDS OF KINDNESS

Scatter seeds of kindness
Everywhere you go;
Scatter bits of courtesy—
Watch them grow and grow.
Gather buds of friendship;
Keep them till full blown.
You will find more happiness
Than you have ever known.
Gather every bit of love
All that you can find,
With it bind the broken hearts
For love heals all mankind.
—Amy K. Raabe

Be kind to your family. They like to see your good side the same as the rest of the world.

One time a mother had developed the habit of being cross and unkind to her children. Away from home she was all sweetness and light. One night after she had been especially cross she heard her little child praying.

"Dear God, make mommie love me like she does the people we visit."

The woman thought at first the prayer was funny. She told it to her husband in the living room. He looked at her with a solemn face.

"You do not treat us with the courtesy you show to the tradespeople, to your friends, or even to the maid."

She was ashamed of her poor treatment of her family and tried to make her life sweeter toward them.

A forgiving heart makes for a beautiful spirit. Be first to forgive. That is one time it is good to be first. Christ found it easy to forgive, yet the price he paid for our forgiveness was very high.

The most beautiful person is the one who has the inner glow of Christ's love shining through his life at all times.

Let Christ's beauty shine through me,
For all the whole wide world to see.

69

18

Look at Christmas!

"When they saw the star, they rejoiced with exceeding great joy." — Matthew 2:10

Long ago Eugene Field wrote the following Christmas poem.

STAR OF THE EAST

Star of the East, that long ago brought wise
    men on their way
Where, angels singing to and fro, the child
    of Bethlehem lay—
Above the Syrian hill afar thou shinest out
    to-night, O Star!
Star of the East, the night were drear, but
    for the tender grace
That with thy glory comes to cheer earth's
    loneliest, darkest place;
For by that charity we see where there is
    hope for all and me.
Star of the East show us the way, in wisdom
    undefiled.
To seek that manger out and lay our gifts
    before the child—
To bring our hearts and offer them unto our
    King in Bethlehem.

               —Eugene Field

LOOK AT CHRISTMAS!

Looking at my list of things to be bought, of cards to be written, and tasks to be accomplished, I noticed on the very last line these words, "Look at Christmas."

Look at Christmas. I had planned to just take some time downtown and look in all the stores, look at all the expensive decorations, look at all the new gadgets invented to cause people to spend money.

The city was just as I expected, only more so. The streets were crowded with people. The stores were tempting in their gorgeous arrays of gifts. The Court House was decorated with expensive tinsel and bells. Across the street ropes of lights and tinsel were hanging for many blocks.

Late that night I returned home exhausted. Opening my purse I saw my crumpled piece of paper with my list written on it. Glancing over the list I saw once again the words, "Look at Christmas." Suddenly I was ashamed, not just of myself but of my town and my world. We were not looking at Christmas; we were looking at a commercial extravaganza. Where was Christ in all that rush and show?

Christmas has become one of the greatest holidays of the Protestant, Catholic, and Greek churches. The origin of the celebration of Christmas is uncertain — who first celebrated it, where, or how. We do not even know the exact date of Christ's birth.

Christmas, look at Christmas — how much this day should mean to every Christian. Sad to say it is often desecrated.

A small child was said to have quoted John 3:16 as follows: "For God so loved the world, that he gave his only 'forgotten' son, that whosoever believeth in him should not perish, but have everlasting life."

What place should we give Jesus when we plan the celebration of His birthday? How wrong I was to look for Christmas in the shops and stores of a big city.

If I would find Christmas I must first think of the one for whom it was established. Think of the millions who have yet to hear about Christ. So I cannot close my home and leave

71

my family to go to foreign lands and look for Christmas; but I can make a gift of money to help someone who wants to go to a mission field.

Because there are hungry people in our city, I cannot say, "We will not eat." However, I can take food to the needy and helpless.

So when you get ready to look for Christmas there are some plans we might make.

Enthrone Christ in your heart and think first of Him on the anniversary of His birth.

Plan to worship Christ. The men from the East fell down before the child and worshiped Him. We too need to worship our Saviour and Lord.

We must worship Christ in our homes as well as at church. We can begin by worshiping in song. Is there any sweeter music in the world than the Christmas hymns. How little children love Luther's Cradle Hymn, long before they can pronounce all the words!

Plan to have a program in your home in connection with the giving of gifts. The time is just right for reading the Christmas story from the Bible.

We cannot truly worship and serve God if we use His birthday as an excuse to go to excess in buying gifts. The old saying so many people fall back upon, "Christmas comes but once a year," was not born in heaven. It is no excuse for wild orgies of spending, eating, and drinking.

The men from the East brought what they had to Jesus as gifts. We can go out and look for Christmas and find many people and places where help is needed.

A college girl was up at dawn on Christmas morning to go with the Goodfellows and distribute food and gifts to poor families. She saw little children sleeping on thin quilts on the floor; she saw houses with no floors except the dirt. Her life will never be quite the same after having seen the gratitude of those poor parents.

How much better to be the one who is able to share with those in need, than to be the one in want!

LOOK AT CHRISTMAS!

MY CHRISTMAS LIST

Have you made your Christmas list, thought of
    every one?
Grandpa, grandma, mother, dad, daughter, too,
    and son?
Have you made your Christmas list? Giving is
    in the air!
Nieces, nephews, uncles, aunts, friends from
    everywhere.
Have you made your list? Yes beyond a doubt!
It is Jesus' birthday, too. Did you leave
    him out?
Make his gift the first of all "Inasmuch as ye
Did it to the least of mine, ye did it unto me."
Christmas gift to all the world—dearest, finest,
    first and best!
When I make my Christmas list, his name leads
    the rest.

—Edith G. Step

Look at Christmas! A family day, a happy day, a day we
long have cherished. So let us see the good we can do for
others as we help them to know our Saviour.

19

One Day at a Time

"Take therefore no thought for the morrow; for the morrow shall take thought for the things of itself. Sufficient unto the day is the evil thereof."

— *Matthew 6:34*

Look to this day!
For it is life, the very life of life.
In its brief course lie all the varieties
   and realities of your existence;
The bliss of growth:
The glory of action:
The splendor of beauty:
For yesterday is already a dream,
   and tomorrow is only a vision:
But today, well lived, makes every yesterday
A dream of happiness, and every tomorrow
   a vision of hope.
Look well, therefore, to this day!

Someone has aptly said; "Never bear more than one trouble at a time."

Some people bear three kinds — all they have ever had, all they have now, and all they expect to have.

Some people are like the little boy who did not recognize

trouble when it came. The teacher was very angry and called him to the desk.

"This essay on 'Our Horse' is word for word like your brother's."

Billy looked at her in a disgusted way; "Well you see it's the same horse."

How we clutter up our days by worry over things which might happen in the future. During a sick spell one time I entertained myself by thinking back over all the things I had been troubled about which never happened. Some looked vrey foolish and funny as I looked back at them through the glasses of time.

We must learn to think of one day at a time. If all the dishes I will wash the rest of my life were stacked in a room, I would want to lock the door and throw away the key. With time to wash them day by day, washing dishes seems a small task.

If all the gasoline a man will burn from the age of twenty-one until he is too old to drive, could be put in one huge tank in our town, we would run away in fear. Isn't it fun burning it just one tank at a time?

When you are asked to serve the Lord by taking an office in the church, or asked to visit, I am afraid we too often look at the whole task for the year and refuse. If we would only have faith, and accomplish our tasks one day at a time.

When we were young and in love, if we could have seen all the hardships of the years to come in one big picture, we would have been afraid to marry, and so have missed the joy of working out life's problems with a companion, one day at a time.

> For this one day alone, dear God, I pray:
> Help me to walk the straight and narrow way
>   With cheerful mind;
> Help me to think, to act, the golden rule,
> To do my best with book or beast or tool,
>   To serve mankind.

Help me to think before I speak a word
That might by chance, hurt one who overheard,
   And make him sad;
Help me to laugh with clean and wholesome mirth,
To scorn the thought that evil minds give birth,
   or actions bad.

Help me to see in sunshine and in rain,
In daylight and in dark, thy hand again,
   Thy love alone;
And then at eve, when work is put away,
Help me, dear Lord, to lift my eyes and say,
   "Thy will be done."

                       —Selected

When we think of the chaos in our world today, we are so troubled. The world looks so big and the problems so complex. Yet it is my duty and your duty to look at our own corner of the world. My particular world is a modest home sitting on a city lot. Each day I hope to make it an oasis of love and joy for my family. I want to make the world of my home a place where troubles are shared, where life is sweet, and God is honored.

To live just for our own home is not enough. We must lift our eyes to the people around us. We have a responsibility to our schools, our churches, all the institutions in our towns. One step at a time as we are called on, we can help make our world a better place in which to live.

At a lovely wedding I spoke to the mother of the bride. "How proud you must be of your daughter; she is so pretty and poised."

"I am proud of her in many ways," she told me. "Four years ago a judge called and asked if we would give a teen-age girl a home for a few days."

She told me the story of taking in the girl who had absolutely no place to go. Given the privilege of attending school she proved to have a bright mind. She finished well ahead of the majority of her class. The boy she was marrying was a fine young man and her future looked bright.

ONE DAY AT A TIME

"I took care of her problems just one day at a time." My friend seemed so happy. "I learned to sew and counsel, and above all share love with a child who had never known love."

Oh the joy that woman will have when she stands before her Master in the final judgment and hears Him say, "Well done."

If every Christian would start today to do a bit for God's glory, then tomorrow it would be easy to do a little more for His kingdom.

BURDENS OF TOMORROW

God broke our years into hours and days,
That hour by hour, and day by day,
Just going on a little way,
　　We must be able, all along,
　　　To keep quite strong.
Should all the weight of life be laid
Across the future, rife with woe and struggle,
Meet us face to face:
We could not go;
Our feet would stop, and so
God lays a little on us every day.
And never, I believe, in all life's way,
　　Will burdens bear so deep,
　　　Or pathways lie so steep,
But we can go, if by God's power,
We only bear the burden of the hour.
　　　　　　　　　　　—Selected

20

A Master Plan

"Train up a child in the way he should go: and when he is old, he will not depart from it." — Proverbs 22:6

One time I went to visit a young couple with their first baby. They were so elated over the little one. For them all of life had taken on a new purpose and meaning.

"We are not making much salary now, but we started a savings account for the baby." I later found out the savings account consisted of putting two dollars a week in a savings and loan bank, in the baby's name. "When he is ready for college his savings account will see him through the first two years."

That young couple had already formed a master plan for bringing up their little bundle of heaven. They knew he would need a college education and although they were poor, they planned so he would get the training he needed — all before he had his first tooth or could say one word about his own desires.

A good carpenter would not go out to build a chicken coop without a plan in mind to go by. A home owner plans for days before he turns his plans over to a builder. Anything worth building is worth planning first.

A MASTER PLAN

God made plans for us. What a dark world this would be if God had not planned a way of redemption for sinful man!

Most organizations plan their work a year in advance, then strive to carry out those plans.

So we need to make a master plan for our lives and for the lives of our children.

The foundation of our life's plan should be a Christian home. It should be a place where God is honored and worshiped, a place where God is called upon in daily prayer to guide and direct our every activity.

Have you ever traveled in California? Many places in the large cities are built upon the sides of the hills. They seem to have very little foundation. I was not surprised to read in the paper about some houses sliding off the sides of the hills.

How often when a child grows up and gets into trouble, do we say, "Well, look at the way he has lived all his life."

After the foundation of a Chirstian home comes the framework of a life built on church attendance. Judges tell us they have fewer children in court from Christian homes. So having the high ideals of the church built into life's plan makes a strong framework.

"Train up a child in the way he should go."

When someone has made a famous name for himself, either in a good way or a bad, we are interested in the type of childhood that person had. We wonder about his friendships.

Many a mother has sadly said of her child, "He or she got in bad company."

Any person young or old needs to fill in his foundation and framework with friends. Many a man has gotten a job because of his friends. We have all heard the trite old saying: "Not what you know, but who you know."

As parents we need to plan for our children to know people who are honest and true, people who live the kind of lives we want to live, and want our children to live.

A friendship can change a life; a friendship can change the world. Think of Jesus and John. Think of Paul and Timothy. Think of the friendship of God and Abraham.

The kind of friends we choose and the kind we allow our children to choose has a great deal of influence on our master plan for life.

My husband had an uncle who had a motto: "Rub shoulders with all the big men you can; some of it will rub off on you."

"According to your faith be it done unto you." Jesus spoke these words. What can be better to tie a master plan together than faith. Faith in God, faith in fellowman, faith in the future. There is no limit to God's power in meeting our needs in life if we only have faith.

There are many other things we need to put into our master plan for the lives of our children and ourselves. We would never want to leave out a plan for hope, for optimism, for music, for love of beauty.

What a responsibility, and what a privilege to have a part in planning for someone's life and happiness.

We must never forget there is a master builder who oversees all things. The ruler in Egypt thought he had a plan to destroy all potential leaders. God had a plan to save the great leader, Moses. No master plan of ours can succeed if we fail to depend upon God for directions.

My life is but a weaving
Between my Lord and me.
I cannot choose the colors
Nor all the pattern see;
Sometimes he chooseth sorrow
And I, in foolish pride,
Forget he sees the upper
And I the lower side.

Not till the loom is silent,
And the shuttles cease to fly,
Will he reveal the pattern,
Or tell the reason why
The dark threads are so needful
In the weaver's skillful hand,
As the threads of gold and silver
In the pattern he has planned.

21

Strings across Our Lives

". . . let us lay aside every weight, and the sin which doth so easily beset us, and let us run with patience the race that is set before us." — Hebrews 12:1

Late one fall afternoon I noticed some children flying kites in my backyard. They were having so much fun. Then, as so often happens with kites, the strings became tangled and the kites landed in the elm tree. I was too busy to go out and help untangle the strings, and so dismissed the children from my mind. Next morning when I went to the kitchen window the yard had completely changed. It looked as if the snow fairies had come during the night. The ground was covered with the first snow of the season. Across the yard, about five feet above the ground, were the kite strings all covered with snow. With the kite strings, the clothes lines, and the light and telephone wires all running across the yard, all covered with snow and ice — well, my yard looked like a giant package some child had tried to wrap. As I stood gazing out the window the thought of strings across our lives came to me.

When we first see the strings across our lives we think, "That must not be allowed to stay; it is a bad habit. I'll see about it tomorrow."

Then tomorrow comes and if we are not careful the habit is ignored or forgotten because something or someone has covered it with snow and from the inside it looks beautiful.

One of the first strings to come across anyone's life is usually telling fibs. Maybe a child tells just a little story to keep from getting a spanking. Maybe a grown person tells just a little untruth to keep from hurting someone. The habit of fibbing just a little gets to be a string wrapped across our lives and many times never torn away and destroyed.

When I was just a very small child, my father had a cobbling outfit. At night he worked on people's shoes for extra money. The tools fascinated me, and often when he was away during the day I would play with them. One day I broke the awl. I was very frightened. Taking the tool to the back door I threw it just as far as I could. That night when my dad started to work on shoes he could not find his awl.

"Have you been in my tools?" he asked me.

"No, I haven't." I knew if I told the truth I would be punished.

Nothing more was said, but next day my dad found his broken tool in the yard. This time he made me tell the truth. The spanking I received was for the story I told. I still remember that lesson well today.

Another string which often stretches across our lives early is taking something which does not belong to us. There is a flower in a yard and it looks just ready to pull; or there is a toy left untended in the street. Then as we grow older there are larger things. So many times people seem to develop the attitude that it is fine to take something they want if no one sees them.

A man told me the story of his first try at stealing. He was playing in a neighbor's yard while his mother visited. He found a knife on the ground. He had never owned a pocket knife; so he wanted it very much. Putting the knife in his pocket he kept it. After they reached home he took the knife out of his pocket and began to see what he could cut. His mother was horrified when she found him cutting things. She asked so many questions about the knife he had to tell her where he had found it.

In those days people grew peach trees for just such occasions. They never heard of juvenile delinquents. The mother cut a long switch from the peach tree and gave the boy a good switching. Then she made him walk back to the neighbors and return the knife.

If parents would always be quick to cut the strings of stealing from their children's lives, they would have less trouble with them after they are grown.

Then, often early in life come the strings of evil habits. I knew a man who had the nasty habit of chewing tobacco. He wanted very much to break the habit but was never strong enough. He had started chewing when he was just eight or nine years old. He and his older brothers worked in the tobacco patches in Tennessee. The older boys would always have a twist of tobacco in their pockets. They would offer it to the little boys because it was good sport to watch them turn green and be sick. But the habit once established was never broken.

The string of laziness attaches itself to people early in life, if they do not tear it away and overcome it. A new bride is tempted to lie in bed and let her house work go. A young man is tempted to go fishing when he should get a summer job. Parents have an obligation to teach their children to work. There cannot be a family rich enough to rob their child of the right to the joy of work well done.

A PRAYER

I am but one; my power is very small;
But take me, use me, till setting sun,
Thou who art all in all.
I am so frail, too weak to contemplate;
But thou art mighty and can avail to make
my smallness great.

—Thomas Clark

There are strings of jealousy, envy, hate, and meanness. These can be torn away when they first start wrapping themselves around a child's life. When they have grown through the years they can be torn away only by a changed heart coming from trust in Christ.

22

You May Be Rich

"A good name is rather to be chosen than great riches,
and loving favor rather than silver and gold."
— *Proverbs 22:1*

A PRAYER

It is my joy in life to find
　　At every turning of the road,
The strong arm of a comrade kind
　　To help me onward with my load.
And since I have no gold to give,
　　And love alone must make amends,
My only prayer is, while I live—
　　God make me worthy of my friends.
　　　　　　　　　—Selected

One lovely spring day I started out to make some calls for my church. I had a list of names and addresses. The first address turned out to be an antique shop. Now I am too poor to indulge in buying antiques, but any woman likes to indulge in looking. The shop seemed to be empty when I entered but I just walked around and gazed at the beautiful things.

"Did you wish something?" a kind voice spoke.

Looking toward the back I saw a man seated behind a desk. "Yes, I wanted to find a Mrs. Lucy King."

"You must have the wrong address, I live here and run this shop. My name is Needmore." He seemed to be such a kind person.

"I copied the name and address right on this paper." I felt rather foolish.

"Why don't you look in my phone book. There must be a mistake." He motioned me toward the phone.

With my usual carelessness I had made an error of ten blocks copying the number. I apologized and started for the door.

"I wish I could sell you some antiques. You seem to like them so much," he said as I started to leave.

"Oh, I wish you could, but I am too poor for antiques." I smiled back at him.

"You may be richer than you think," he told me. Then for the first time I noticed he was sitting in a wheel chair and not a desk chair.

On two strong legs I ran out to my little car. I did not mind in the least that it was ten years old. I was rich, I could go where I pleased under my own steam. As I drove the ten blocks my heart kept singing over and over, "You may be richer than you think."

At the next place I found a young mother with two small children. They seemed so glad to have a visitor from the church.

"We are only getting our furniture a piece at a time," the young woman told me. "The room looks a little bare."

"What is furniture when you have so many riches?" I told her about my experience in the antique shop. As I was leaving I said to her, "With your fine strong husband and your pretty children, you are richer than you think."

Driving along making my visits I passed a large house, very fine and pretentious looking. I knew the father in that home had served a prison term for fraud. The thought of the shame and humiliation the family had suffered made me think of our Scripture.

"A good name is rather to be chosen."

The person who is given a good name by his family has received a rich heritage. We have no choice about the name we are born with, but we can be grateful when it is one we can be proud of. A child born with a tarnished name has a strike against him before he starts out in life.

We have all been told so many times that it is a trite statement, but we are richer than we can ever realize because we were born in America. On rare occasions during my lifetime I have read about people who disliked the United States as a native land so much they renounced citizenship.

My heart would find only contempt and pity for such people. They were richer than they thought.

A boy, who had the privilege of being sent for six weeks as an ambassador of good will to a foreign country, told me this experience.

When he arrived at his destination he was met by the family he was to live with. The son of the family as soon as possible asked him if he had a car. In a rather embarrassed way he answered. "Well, I have an old car. It is seven years old."

"I knew it!" exclaimed his host. "You are one of those rich Americans."

Because even a seven year old car would cost around $5,000.00 in their country, they felt their guest must be rich. He could never make them understand that almost any boy who wanted to work after school could afford an old car.

"Do you know how rich you are? Have you stopped to count all the things you possess, which money cannot buy?"

When I look at little children playing on the school ground, I want to shout to them, "Do you know how rich you are?"

Our children are so rich, in heritage, in opportunities, in freedoms.

23

Linings of Silver

"And the king made silver to be in Jerusalem as stones, and cedars made he to be as the sycamore trees that are in the vale, for abundance." — I Kings 10:27

Once while waiting at the airport for a big plane to land I overheard a small child say:

"Oh mommie look! The plane is lined with silver!"

At least a dozen people waiting there in the bright sunshine gave an extra glance toward the plane. A number of them smiled and spoke to the little girl.

Many times I had been there to meet that same plane but never before had I given a thought to the way the aluminum shone in the sun, in resemblance to silver.

"Would you like to ride in a silver plane?" a young man asked the child.

"I can ride when I play make believe." Her reply was satisfactory to the young man. He was not too old to remember when he too played "make believe."

Then I asked myself the question, Do we see all the lovely silver linings to the days we are allowed to live? We spend so much time looking for something to complain about, we fail to see all the lovely little blessings with which our days are lined. We often let our days glide by without noticing the happy things.

When dark days come and the clouds are black we look back and remember how happy and beautiful were the days we just took for granted.

COUNT YOUR BLESSINGS

When upon life's billows you are tempest tossed,
When you are discouraged, thinking all is lost,
Count your many blessings, name them one by one,
And it will surprise you what the Lord hath done.
—Joseph Oatman, Jr.

A mother insisted that each child and grandchild be present for a family reunion. A few days after the reunion the father of the clan died, with a heart attack.

"Oh mother, we are so glad we had that day with dad," a daughter tearfully expressed the feelings of the children.

"Yes, we are all glad now. I knew he had only a short time to live," the mother smiled. "Now all of you have a shining happy day to remember as the last spent with your father."

When I was a small girl, an old fashioned road show came to our town. One of the ladies in the show wore a beautiful white dress, lined with silver. The performance she gave made very little impression on me. The lining of her dress fascinated me. I was determined to have a dress, just like hers, when I grew up.

A young mother with small children to feed, bathe, dress, and sometimes to care for through sickness, often complains: "I'll be so glad when they are old enough to go to school." She fails completely to see the happy side of her days. She does not recognize the precious privilege of holding those dear little ones close to her heart, and keeping them safe from harm.

A middle aged mother whose children are all gone from home looks back and often remarks, "Their childhood days were more happy for me than I realized at the time."

Failure to see the silver linings of our days is not limited to mothers. Men are often heard to complain about their jobs being tiresome or unrewarding. They plan big on the things they will do when they retire. They fail to enjoy the blessing of being strong and able to hold a job. They loose the joy and pride in each day's accomplishments. When the time for retirement comes they look back and think of the happy days they enjoyed as young men building a business, or developing a career. Each person should write a letter to himself at age forty, to be opened at sixty-five. Such a letter might help one to realize his blessings.

SMILE

If you don a little frown
And you wear it all day long
You will find that little frown
Took away your happy song.

Now a smile's a better garb
Than a frown can ever be,
For it lights the hearts of men
And encourages, you see.
    —J. T. Bolding

When I make a dress or window drapes or quilts, I select the lining I want them to have. We can select the silver lining for our days, if we will look at all the pleasant happy things and ignore the little unpleasant happenings.

Every man and woman has the right and privilege of being master of his thoughts and ideals. If we look at things from a bright viewpoint those around us will grow happier.

In the Bible we read of people who were possessed with devils. With the help of Christ they were released from the evil spirits. Where they had been miserable and uncontrollable they became useful and happy. We can have the help of Christ today in casting out the things from our days which make us discouraged and blue. It is up to us to seek, through prayer, the companionship and help of our Lord. If we have Christ for our Saviour, then when troubles or trials cloud

LININGS OF SILVER

our days we can rest in the assurance of Jesus' words, "Lo, I am with you always."

Are the linings of your days made of silver? If you think they are not, look back fifty years or a hundred years. See how much you have to be thankful for. Would you prefer a horse and buggy to a car? Would you prefer uncooled houses to cool air-conditioned ones? Would you prefer the old time ice man to your modern refrigerator? Would you prefer almost certain death, as in some diseases, to the new miracle drugs which can combat those dread infections?

Look at the linings of silver we have in our modern age. They are like the text thoughts, "Silver as stones," where the people had so much silver and cedar they were over abundant. We have so many silver linings we forget to count them as blessings.

SHINING LININGS

Some garments have linings of silver
　　While others have linings of gold;
And some are of fleece or of flannel,
　　With colors, light, drab, bright or bold.

Some linings are used for sheer beauty;
　　While some are for warmth, I am told;
Some serve to give shape to the garment,
　　And some help to keep out the cold.

Has Jesus been filling your life's way
　　With blessings so wondrously fair,
And fitting the burdens you carry
　　To you with His infinite care?

That others may know of His blessings
　　Bestowed upon you every mile,
Just flash out the happiest linings
　　And let them show through in your smile.
　　　　　　　　　　　—J. T. Bolding

24

Some Things
Must Be Watered

*"Now he that planteth and he that watereth are one:
and every man shall receive his own reward according
to his own labor. For we are laborers together with
God: ye are God's husbandry, ye are God's building."*
— I Corinthians 3:8, 9

From April to October I spend a great amount of time
watering my yard. First I turn on the hose in the front yard,
then I go to the back yard. Often during the day the hose
must be moved so each spot of grass or bed of flowers will be
watered. If we go on vacation we must get friends or hired
men to water for us each day. Perhaps dry West Texas is
the only place where so much watering is required. When we
eat breakfast in the back yard and sit looking at the beautiful flowers and shrubs, I never think of all the water they
must take.

So it is with life. There are joys to be had for the person
who is willing to water and care for things each day.

A young man stood to speak in a Sunday School department. He had received some high honors in his high school
and college. He told of his life in school.

SOME THINGS MUST BE WATERED

"I have never taken a step on the dance floor, I have never smoked a cigarette or swallowed a drink of liquor," he told us.

"Is it hard? People ask me." He made a face. "You ain't a woffin," he answered himself in school boy language.

Then he told us his secret. "When I saw what life was like in our school and knew I had pledged not to do those things, I asked God to help me. Like others, I too wanted to be a leader. I felt I had leadership ability, without following all the bad habits of the majority."

He lifted his fine head and looked at our department of middle aged people. "With Christ looking over my shoulder I determined to be a leader in my school and still stay true to my convictions."

That young man was only one in many thousands strong enough to be a leader and yet not be swayed by popular opinion. In order to succeed he had to take great care to cultivate and water certain characteristics.

He had to think unselfishly of others. He had to be a friend to those who were weaker characters than himself. He had to encourage the ones with whom he worked. At all times he must make them feel he was their friend and had their best interest at heart.

He learned to love those who were his enemies and those who spent time making light of his moral standards. It was very hard to stand above the majority of students. His study light must have burned often at night when others were out having fun. When he stood on the platform and received the honor of being elected President of the Student Body he forgot all the sacrifice and work. He had achieved his goal — as he said, "With Christ looking over my shoulder."

If a young couple, when they turn away from the marriage altar to start a home, would only beware of the things which must be watered and tended with care.

There is always the flowerbed of forgiveness. Many homes have been broken and lives shattered because the flower of forgiveness had not been watered and made to grow in their hearts.

If people love, they will more quickly forgive. So of course there must be much care for the flower of love. The happy marriage is one where helpfulness is the border flower in all the days, helpfulness for each other in all the phases of life together.

To be admired is the wife who plans and works to make her husband a pampered king in his own home. Most men when treated in such a manner will work to make the wife happy and be worthy of her love.

Many more things could be named which would be nice to water and grow in our lives, but we need also to pause and give a thought to the things we must not water and encourage to grow.

The ugly weed of selfishness is a spreading menace. Life for the selfish person can never be sweet and happy.

Ambition is a good flower to water; but it so nearly resembles the weed of greed we must look closely and be sure to keep out the greed.

One time I let my flower bed fill up with weeds because I thought they looked like certain kinds of flowers. Almost too late I discovered they were very ugly weeds and hard to destroy. Often in life we waste precious time and effort trying to keep something watered that is only a useless weed. Many friendships are not worth the time and effort they consume. Families should take care to water the flowers of good friendships.

A grandmother who baby-sat for her grandchildren allowed the ten-year-old boy to roam away from home and become friends with a very mean boy. The mother told him never to go to play with that mean boy again.

"I can't see what it would hurt when he is so young." The grandmother defended him.

"Friendships are often lasting," explained the mother. When they are in high school it will be too late to break up a companionship which might lead to bad habits and troubles."

Sometimes others reap the blessings from things we work hard to water. Your children will reap the benefits from your own good planning and care.

YOUR PLACE

Is your place a small place?
Tend it with care;—
He set you there.
Is your place a large place?
Guard it with care!—
He set you there.
Whate'er your place, it is
Not yours alone, but His
Who set you there.
—John Oxenham

25

Planting and Reaping

"They that sow in tears shall reap in joy. He that goeth forth and weepeth, bearing precious seed, shall doubtless come again with rejoicing, bringing his sheaves with him." — Psalm 126:5, 6

Every day you have a handful of seed to plant; each day you reap some harvest from seed already sown.

Let us think of a few of the seeds we plant each day.

The seed of friendship is one we start planting early in life and which we stop planting only when we leave this world. Some people are more adept at making friends than others. Friendship is a seed we should gladly bestow on all who need it.

A school boy was asked for the definition of a friend. He replied, "A friend is a guy who knows you real well but he still likes you."

Many people are not willing to plant the seed of friendship until someone becomes rich or famous; then they like to say, "I knew him when - - - - -."

We should make the most of every opportunity to be a friend, and to make friends. There is one friend of whom the Bible said, "There is a friend who sticketh closer than a brother." This friend we must know better than all others if we would reap life's richest harvest.

Sometimes we see people whose lives have been ruined because they planted the seed of friendship in the wrong places. A good test as to the worthiness of a person's friendship is influence. After an evening spent with a friend is it easy or hard for you to go home and pray? If the answer is hard, then it would be best to weed out that friendship quickly.

Another important seed we have to plant each day of our lives is the seed of love. We have love in our hearts for our parents, our sisters and brothers. We need to tend the love for relatives with care. We need also to grow a love for our creator and Lord. We need to show to the world our love for Him. No one who loves others has lived in vain. Those who love Christ have lived to win others to Christ.

In John 15:13 we read, "Greater love hath no man than this, that a man lay down his life for his friends."

Most famous people did not become famous because they loved themselves; they loved and lived for others. Many had dreams of making the world a better place, and a safer place. They loved others so much they were willing to sacrifice and work hard in order to make their dreams come true.

There is a very important seed called study. If we are to be worthwhile in life we must spend much of our youth studying. The harvest we reap in adult life will often be gauged by the amount of study we do as we go through school.

Two boys left their home to go for an overnight trip in the woods. One boy had studied very hard on his Boy Scout projects. He knew the book almost from memory. The other boy was lazy about studying. During the night a snowstorm came. The boys could not return home next morning as they planned. The boy who had studied used his knowledge to make a better shelter, to snare some game, to build a fire.

"I am glad you studied so much in the Scout book," the

lazy boy remarked. "We would sure be in a fix if I had to care for us."

The world would be in a fix if the lazy people had to keep it going.

When I was a child I often heard the song, "Work for the Night Is Coming." Work is a seed we need to plant early. All children and all grownups need to have some work to do. Old age comes when we can no longer work.

A beautiful young woman told me her father would never give her spending money. She must work for it. When she was still too small for any other task, he would hang his work clothes on the clothes line and she hit them with the broom. He was a brick layer and his clothes had lots of dust and cement in them. She grew to womanhood unafraid of life because she knew how to work with her hands.

A different story is that of a pretty young woman who always heard these words, "You are too pretty to work; run and play." She grew up always dependent on other people, always unsure of life.

There are so many seeds in our hands today we cannot possibly mention them all; but we must not neglect the seed of good health habits. The health habits we plant all through life may mean either a strong healthy body or a frail weak one. Sometimes we start bad habits, thinking we can easily break them, but they are like a spool of thread. One string around our body can be easily broken but string, after string, after string — and soon we are helplessly bound.

Look well to the seeds in your hand and plant them with care, for as you plant so will the harvest be.

THE PACKAGE OF SEED

I paid a dime for a package of seeds,
    And the clerk tossed them out with a flip.
"We've got 'em assorted for every man's needs,"
    He said with a smile on his lip.
"Pansies and poppies and asters and peas!
    Ten cents a package! And pick as you please!"

PLANTING AND REAPING

Now seeds are just dimes to the man in the store,
    And the dimes are the things that he needs;
And I've been to buy them in seasons before,
    But have thought of them merely as seeds;
But it flashed through my mind as I took them this time:
    You have purchased a miracle here for a dime.

You've a dime's worth of power which no man can create;
    You've a dime's worth of life in your hand!
You've a dime's worth of mystery, destiny, fate,
    Which the wisest cannot understand.
In this bright little package, now isnt' it odd?
You've a dime's worth of something known only to God.

These are seeds, but the plants and the blossoms are here
    With their petals of various hues;
In these little pellets, so dry and so queer,
    There is power which no chemist can fuse.
Here is one of God's miracles soon to unfold.
    Thus for ten cents an ounce of Divinity sold!
                                        Edgar A. Guest